▶ YouTubers

DUDE PERFECT

D1709504

JESSICA RUSICK

Checkerboard Library

An Imprint of Abdo Publishing
abdobooks.com

abdobooks.com

Printed in the United States of America, North Mankato, Minnesota
102019
012020

 THIS BOOK CONTAINS RECYCLED MATERIALS

Design: Sarah DeYoung, Mighty Media, Inc.
Production: Mighty Media, Inc.
Editor: Rebecca Felix
Cover Photograph: Noam Galai/Film Magic, Inc./Getty Images
Interior Photographs: AJ Mast/AP Images, p. 19; Alex Trautwig/MLB/Getty Images, p. 9; George Bush Presidential Library and Museum/Flickr, p. 7; Logan Bowles/PGA TOUR/Getty Images, pp. 27, 29 (bottom right); Mighty Media, Inc., p. 17 (top); Mike Mozart/Flickr, p. 23; Shutterstock Images, pp. 8, 11, 16, 17 (middle, bottom), 20, 23 (right), 25 (left, right), 28, 29 (bottom left); Stew Milne/AP Images, pp. 5, 13, 21, 29 (top); Taylor Hill/FilmMagic, Inc./Getty Images, p. 15; Tess_Trunk/iStockphoto, pp. 8, 10, 14, 17, 22, 24, 26, 28, 29

Library of Congress Control Number: 2019943213

Publisher's Cataloging-in-Publication Data
Names: Rusick, Jessica, author.
Title: Dude Perfect / by Jessica Rusick
Description: Minneapolis, Minnesota : Abdo Publishing, 2020 | Series: YouTubers | Includes online resources and index.
Identifiers: ISBN 9781532191800 (lib. bdg.) | ISBN 9781644943588 (pbk.) | ISBN 9781532178535 (ebook)
Subjects: LCSH: YouTube (Firm)--Juvenile literature. | YouTube (Firm)--Juvenile literature. | Internet celebrities--Biography--Juvenile literature. | Internet videos--Juvenile literature. | Sports videos--Juvenile literature. | Television programs--Juvenile literature. | Nickelodeon (Television network)--Juvenile literature.
Classification: DDC 927.91--dc23

Contents

Perfect Dudes

Dude Perfect is a sports entertainment group. It has more than 42 million **subscribers** on YouTube! Dude Perfect is one of the most popular YouTube sports channels. In 2019, it was also YouTube's ninth most-subscribed-to channel overall!

Dude Perfect is made up of five friends. They are Tyler Toney, Garrett Hilbert, Cody Jones, Coby Cotton, and Cory Cotton. Together, these men plan, film, and shoot trick sports shots. These trick shots have made Dude Perfect a **viral** sensation.

But Dude Perfect is about more than just trick shots. The men also promote positivity and family-friendly fun. Through friendship and sports, they strive to make the world a better place.

The Dude Perfect members are YouTube superstars. But they never expected to be famous. The Dude Perfect empire began with five friends playing basketball in a Texas backyard.

THE BLIND HATCHET

NERF ULTIMATE
CYBER HOOP
ALLEY-OOP

THE
ARCHER

THE
BLEA

Dude Perfect has several brand partnerships. The group also produces and sells its own merchandise, including Dude Perfect clothing, sports gear, and more.

College Camaraderie

Before becoming YouTubers, the Dude Perfect members were born and raised in Texas. Tyler Toney was born on March 24, 1989, in Plano, Texas. He was his football team's quarterback at Prosper High School in Prosper, Texas.

Tyler also played basketball in high school. It was on this team that he met Garrett Hilbert. Garrett was also born in Plano, on May 13, 1987. Like Tyler, he too played sports. The two bonded over their similar interests and became friends.

Tyler and Garrett's friendship lasted into college. They both attended Texas A&M University in College Station, Texas. There, the pair sought more friends who shared their interest in sports. They also looked for friends who had a strong faith.

Both Tyler and Garrett were raised in **devout** Christian families. Religion was an important part of their lives. In college, Tyler and Garrett attended bible study groups on **campus**. There, they met fellow students and twin brothers Coby and Cory Cotton.

Members of Dude Perfect perform a trick shot at the Texas A&M University library.

The Cottons were born in The Woodlands, Texas on July 17, 1987. They grew up attending church with their father, who was a pastor. They also loved to play sports.

The twins became good friends with Tyler and Garrett. The group of four decided to become roommates. They planned to rent a house together near their college **campus**.

But the group was about to grow. While playing basketball on campus, the friends met Cody Jones. Cody was born on October 9, 1987, in Plano, Texas. He also grew up going to church and playing sports. Tyler, Garrett, and the twins immediately got along with Cody. They asked him to be their fifth roommate.

When the Dude Perfect members first started doing trick shots in their backyard, they bet one another on who could make certain shots. Whoever lost the bet had to give the winner a sandwich. Garrett was first to bet Tyler couldn't make a trick shot. After 20 attempts, Tyler made the shot. So, Garrett owed him a sandwich!

Though Dude Perfect got its start performing basketball trick shots, the group would soon expand to other sports.

In August 2008, the five friends moved in together. Since they all loved basketball, they bought a basketball hoop for their home's backyard. But their backyard was grassy. This surface didn't allow the friends to **dribble** or play games. Instead, the guys started doing trick shots. This included throwing basketballs at the hoop from extreme heights or angles.

Soon, the group had the idea to make a video of their tricks! They wanted to post it online for family and friends. This would become the first Dude Perfect YouTube video.

"Backyard Edition"

Tyler, Garrett, Cody, and the Cotton twins spent two days in the spring of 2009 filming their video of basketball trick shots. They filmed in their backyard and at a nearby park.

Tyler performed many of the shots. His experience as a quarterback had trained him to throw long distances. Tyler threw baskets while standing far from the hoop. For many shots, Tyler didn't even look at the hoop but still made a basket!

With the video complete, the friends created a YouTube channel. Their friend and cameraman Sean Townsend inspired its name. Sean said "Dude, perfect" while filming his friends' trick shots. The group named their channel after the phrase.

Dude Perfect uploaded their video on April 8, 2009. It is called "Backyard Edition." The group thought their friends and family would watch the video. But strangers did too! Within one week, it had 100,000 views.

As of 2019, "Backyard Edition" had more than 30 million views.

In "Backyard Edition," Tyler also made trick shots from behind his back and while standing on his home's roof!

Dude Perfect was among the first YouTube channels **dedicated** to trick shots. And "Backyard Edition" marked the first time a trick shot video had gone **viral**. Dude Perfect had found a new **niche** on YouTube!

More Shots, New Spots

After "Backyard Edition," Dude Perfect created more videos, performing trick shots in other locations. One filmed on their college **campus** would make the group stars.

Tyler wanted to film inside the Texas A&M football stadium. Stadium staff agreed to let the group use the empty stadium for an afternoon. So, the friends moved their backyard basketball hoop onto the track around the football field.

While shooting this video, Tyler climbed to the stadium's second level of stands. He hurled a basketball down toward the hoop. He made a basket! So, he decided to try another shot, this time from the third level.

Tyler's higher shot took more than one try. But eventually he made a basket. Tyler threw the ball from so far away that it stayed in the air for 3.9 seconds before going into the hoop.

Tyler has made countless baskets during trick shots. In later Dude Perfect videos, he makes baskets using footballs and other objects.

Dude Perfect uploaded the video of stadium shots on September 17, 2009. They titled it "World's Longest Basketball Shot." In under 9 hours, the video had 3 million views! Dude Perfect was a YouTube sensation.

Trick Shot Triumphs

Dude Perfect's YouTube popularity led to **debuts** on other platforms. The group was interviewed and featured on several sports-themed news and entertainment shows. These included *ESPN E:60*, *First Take*, and *Around the Horn*.

As Dude Perfect grew more popular, the group's tricks grew more **complicated**. Dude Perfect's first videos featured mainly basketball trick shots. In 2011 and 2012, the friends began featuring trick shots in other sports too, such as football and archery.

In one trick, Tyler threw a football through a target on the back of a moving truck! In the future, the group's videos would feature extreme shots in even more sports, such as baseball and bowling.

Dude Perfect's unofficial sixth member is a person in a panda suit. The panda has appeared in some videos since 2010. Its identity is still a mystery to fans!

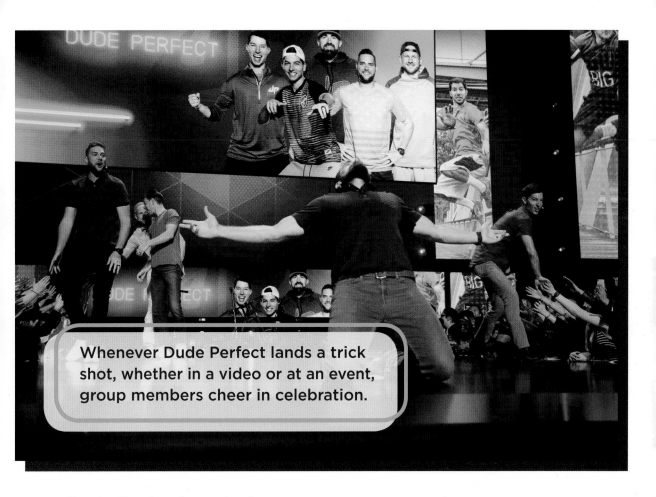

Whenever Dude Perfect lands a trick shot, whether in a video or at an event, group members cheer in celebration.

Dude Perfect's trick shots were so extreme that some viewers thought the performances were faked. Dude Perfect took this reaction as a compliment. The group was proud to pull off tricks so amazing they seemed unbelievable.

Dude Perfect posts to YouTube are polished. But it takes the group a lot of work to perform and film each one. Many tricks

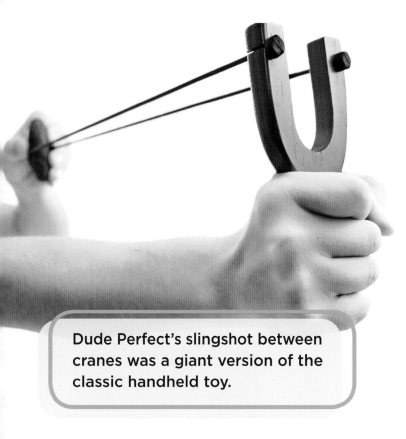

took at least two or three attempts. Some took even longer. One **slingshot** trick took Dude Perfect two full days of shooting to get right.

For this trick, the group strung a giant slingshot between two large **cranes**. Then they shot a basketball from the slingshot into

Dude Perfect's slingshot between cranes was a giant version of the classic handheld toy.

a hoop! The hoop was on the back of a moving vehicle being driven by Cody.

No matter how extreme, most Dude Perfect videos include more than one trick shot. And all videos are edited to present the tricks with a background of upbeat music.

Dude Perfect members also **incorporate** their philosophy, "Go Big," in all their videos. This means being excited, inspiring others, and believing in yourself.

New Channels

Books: In 2011, Cory Cotton published *Go Big: Make Your Shot Count in the Connected World.* The book tells Dude Perfect's story. It also shares the group's secrets to success.

Apps: In 2011, Dude Perfect released a gaming app of the same name. In 2015, the group released *Dude Perfect 2.* In both games, players control Dude Perfect characters to make digital trick shots.

TV: *The Dude Perfect Show* aired on the cable network CMT in 2016. In addition to tricks, the show featured footage of each Dude Perfect member's daily life. The show's second season aired on children's network Nickelodeon, with more seasons planned.

Creating appropriate content was also important to Dude Perfect. The group earned many child fans. Its members wanted to make content that was family-friendly and fun. Promoting positivity became part of the Dude Perfect brand.

Paid Posts

Amid their rise to YouTube stardom, the Dude Perfect members continued their college education. Cody, Garrett, and the Cottons graduated college in 2010. Tyler graduated the following year.

After college, Tyler worked for a **landscaping** company. Garrett worked at an **architecture** company and Cody in real estate. Cory and Coby worked at their father's church. The friends kept busy filming new videos after work and on weekends.

The more popular they became, the greater pressure Dude Perfect members felt to provide fans with content. The guys talked about quitting their jobs to work on Dude Perfect full-time. But to do this, their videos needed to earn them money.

To start earning money from their videos, Dude Perfect set up **sponsorships** from companies. The companies worked with Dude Perfect to create videos with branded content.

Cody shoots for a basket at a 2012 basketball event. As Dude Perfect's fame grew, brands and companies paid members to attend and be featured at events.

Branded content is a type of **marketing**. It places products, logos, or mentions of a brand in videos consumers are already watching for fun. Companies hope seeing stars use or discuss brands will make viewers interested in those brands.

In 2013, the toy brand Nerf partnered with Dude Perfect for a video called "Nerf Blasters Edition." Nerf paid Dude Perfect to use Nerf Blasters in a variety of tricks. In one trick, Cody fired a Nerf dart in the air. Then he caught it in a cup that was strapped to his head!

Nerf Blasters come in many varieties and sizes.

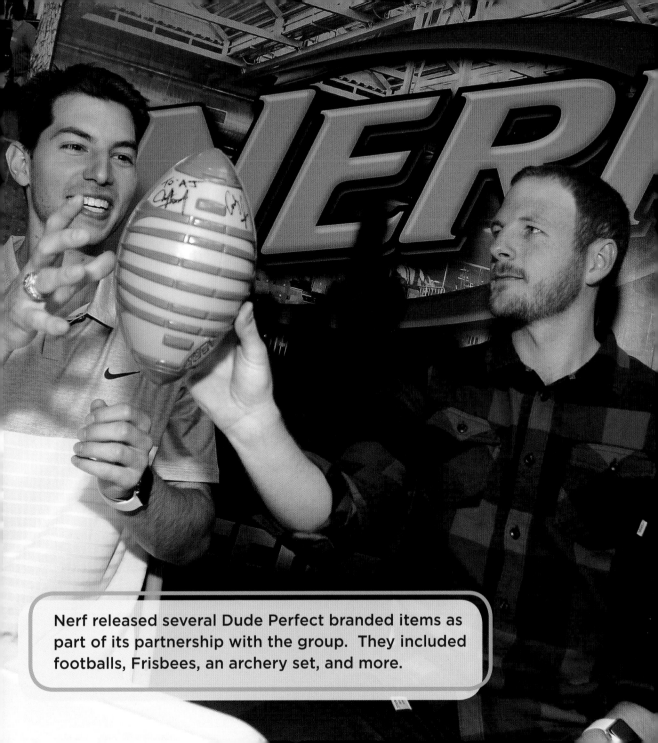

Nerf released several Dude Perfect branded items as part of its partnership with the group. They included footballs, Frisbees, an archery set, and more.

Giving It a Shot

Dude Perfect secured more and more branded content **sponsorships** in coming years. This included with sports drink company Gatorade and snack food company Pringles.

By 2014, Dude Perfect was earning enough sponsorship money that its members felt comfortable making filming their career. They quit their jobs to focus on Dude Perfect full-time!

The group turned an office in Frisco, Texas, into the Dude Perfect headquarters (DPHQ). They outfitted it with basketball hoops, a ping-pong table, a dart board, and a **putting green**. Dude Perfect began shooting many of its videos at DPHQ.

VIP Post

Dude Perfect's most popular video is called "Ping Pong Trick Shots 3." It's a compilation of trick shots featuring ping-pong balls. The video has more than 200 million views! In one trick, Cody throws a ping-pong ball into a cup attached to a moving Frisbee.

In addition to brands, Dude Perfect also began featuring famous athletes in videos. In 2014, the group filmed with football star Russell Wilson. In 2016, tennis star Serena Williams joined Dude Perfect to shoot tennis trick shots.

By this time, Dude Perfect had more than 5 million **subscribers**. As the group's fan base and partnerships continued to expand, so did their ideas for content.

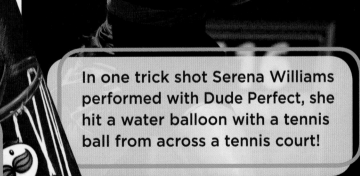

In one trick shot Serena Williams performed with Dude Perfect, she hit a water balloon with a tennis ball from across a tennis court!

Part of Dude Perfect's Pringles sponsorship included special chip cans.

Breaking Records

In 2013, Dude Perfect expanded into new content areas to gain even more fans. That year, Stereotypes **debuted** on the group's YouTube channel. Videos in this series poke fun at the way people act during common activities, such as playing sports. In 2015, the group debuted Battles. This video series features group members competing against one another in sports-themed contests.

VIP Post

Dude Perfect broke several Guinness World Records in their video "World Record Edition." Garrett accomplished the longest blindfolded hook shot and Cody the world's longest sitting basketball shot. Tyler broke the record for world's highest basketball shot. He made a basket from 533 feet (162 m) in the air, while standing on top of a building! The basket was at the base of the building.

One record Dude Perfect broke in "Football World Record Edition" was the highest football pass ever caught. For this record, Cody threw a football from a helicopter. Tyler caught it from 563 feet (172 m) below!

The next year, Dude Perfect took on another challenge. In the 8-minute-long "World Record Edition," the group broke 11 Guinness World Records! In 2017, it broke 14 more in "Football World Record Edition."

Dude Perfect also broke records unrelated to sports. In 2018, this included the farthest distance walking on LEGO bricks barefoot. In addition to setting records, Dude Perfect earned more fame and fans with every post.

Up Next

By August 2017, Dude Perfect had 20 million **subscribers**. The group continued to provide fans with new content. In January 2018, the first episode of Dude Perfect's new YouTube series, Overtime, launched.

Overtime followed a talk show format. In each episode, Dude Perfect members discuss sports and other topics that interest them.

In April 2019, Dude Perfect announced the Pound It Noggin Tour. The tour would visit 20 US cities. Its title refers to a phrase from Dude Perfect videos. "Pound it. Noggin!" is what the guys say as they give one another a fist bump and a head bump! Each show on the tour will involve Dude Perfect doing live tricks and meeting fans.

In 2016, DPHQ moved to a larger space in Frisco. It featured a full-sized basketball court, hockey rink, mini soccer field, gym, and more.

Young Dude Perfect fans wait to meet the group at a Florida golf event in March 2019.

From YouTube to television, apps to tours, fans around the world keep watching Dude Perfect. By summer 2019, the group's YouTube **subscriber** count reached more than 43 million. Dude Perfect's positivity and skills stand to earn the group continued success. Pound it. Noggin!

Timeline

1987

Garrett Hilbert, Cory Cotton, Coby Cotton, and Cody Jones are born in Texas.

2009

Dude Perfect uploads "Backyard Edition" to YouTube in April. In one week, the video has more than 100,000 views.

2010

Garrett, Cody, and the Cotton twins graduate college.

1989

Tyler Toney is born in Texas.

2009

In September, Dude Perfect uploads "World's Longest Basketball Shot." The video goes viral, getting 3 million views in under 9 hours.

2011

Tyler graduates college.

2014

Dude Perfect members quit their jobs to become full-time YouTube stars. They move into their first official headquarters in Frisco, Texas.

2018

Dude Perfect launches a YouTube talk show series called Overtime.

2016

Dude Perfect begins a trend of breaking Guinness World Records in videos.

2019

Dude Perfect announces the Pound It Noggin Tour, which will visit 20 US cities.

Glossary

architecture—the art of planning and designing buildings.

campus—the grounds and buildings of a school.

complicated—having elaborately combined parts.

crane—a machine with cables and a long arm that is used for moving heavy items.

debut (DAY-byoo)—a first appearance. To debut is to first appear or to present or perform something for the first time.

dedicate—to give a lot of time and energy to something.

devout—devoted to religion and religious activities, such as worship and prayer.

dribble—to continually bounce a basketball with one hand.

incorporate—to include or work into.

landscaping—the improving of the natural beauty of an area of land.

marketing—the process of advertising or promoting something so people will want to buy it.

niche (NIHCH)—a place, job, or use for which someone or something is well-suited.

putting green—the smooth grassy area around a hole into which a player aims a golf ball.

slingshot—a Y-shaped device with an elastic band attached that is used to launch rocks or other objects.

sponsorship—a relationship in which a company pays for a program or activity in return for the promotion of the company's product or a brand.

subscriber—someone who signs up to receive something on a regular basis.

viral—quickly or widely spread, usually by electronic communication.

Online Resources

Index